Published by:
Chartsearch Ltd
14 Willow St
London EC2A 4BH



Michael Coleman

ISBN 1-85295-036-6

# How To Write Competition Slogans That Win

Previously published by
Byword Publications
under ISBN 0-9515937-0-6



A Chartsearch Publication

# Contents



Throughout the book you will see a number of **sidebars** like this. They're used to highlight key points.

They also enable you to speed-read through the book for a quick 'refresher' course whenever you need it.

Chapters 4 to 7 are ...

## Chapter 4 . . . . . . . . . . . . . . . p 23

### Successful slogan-writing must begin with what you are given because ...

... what you're given tells you the answers!! The preamble to every slogan competition has hidden **key-words** that the judges will be expecting your slogan to build on. Unlock those key-words and you're on the way to a slogan the judges are almost certain to like - because it's what they've already told you they're looking for!

... illustrated by ...

## Chapter 5 . . . . . . . . . . . . . . . p 32

### You <u>can</u> complete whatever sentence you're given in an apt and original way because ...

... The **key-words** you've found have given you a flying start. But they're the judge's words. You've got to find your own now. Apt and original words. Words that make catchy slogans. How? By using a power method used by some of the most inventive people in industry and commerce: **brainstorming** on those key-words will take you from having maybe one or two ideas to having so many that your problem becomes choosing which ones to throw away!

... a complete example ...

## Chapter 6 . . . . . . . . . . . . . . . p 43

### You have plenty of slogan ideas and word-plays now because ...

... the brainstorming process produces stacks of possible ideas, all of which have the ingredients the judges will be looking for. With another simple technique you can generate the basics for eye-catching word-plays.

... taken step-by-step from scratch.



You may also have noticed some sidebars on the title page. One in particular mentions the fact that copying this book in any way is not allowed without the written permission of the publishers.

Please respect this, and remember ... a **'photo' for you is a 'negative' for us!**

# 1

## Being able to write good slogans is important because ...

... if you're really serious about trying to win competitions then you need a way of coming up with good, catchy slogans ten times out of ten.

Why?

**Competitors Companion** is published monthly by **Chartsearch Ltd, 14 Willow Street, London EC2A 4BH**

Look at the competitions advertised in any newspaper or magazine. Look at the competition details given in *Competitor's Companion.* The chances are that about 60% of those competitions - 3 out of every 5 - will be asking you to write a slogan of some sort.

Some of them will be straight 'write-a-slogan' competitions. Others, and this is a favourite format, will be asking you to answer a few questions first, and then come up with a slogan which will be used as a tie-breaker. But think about it. The questions are often pretty easy - deliberately, so that plenty of people will be tempted to enter.

On top of that, the editors of *Competitor's Companion* will be suggesting the likeliest answers to its many subscribers. All of which means that there are going to be plenty of ties! The effect? In practice, all question-and-answer competitions actually boil down to slogan competitions in the end!

### So why are there so many slogan competitions?

Well, there are plenty of reasons and it's important for a serious comper to bear them in mind. You will find that they surface time and time again as we go through this book.

Slogans ...

- A slogan competition gets you - the competitor - to think good things about a particular product. Don't forget, inside every competition there's an advertisement trying to get out. The promoters of the competition are after your custom, and they get it by asking you to send proofs of purchase and the like with your entry. But, in addition to that, they want you to think favourably about their product. And what better way than to get you to write such good thoughts down in the form of a slogan!

.. get you thinking positive thoughts

- **Slogans sell!** Competition winners are publicised - and so are their winning slogans. So when that brilliant slogan of yours is announced, it's going to get every other comper thinking well of the promoter's product too. Advertising is what it's all about!

... get others thinking the same way

- Slogans really are the perfect tie-breaker. In theory, every slogan sent in could be different. (In practice, this isn't the case - and it's a pitfall we'll be looking at in the next chapter. If your slogan isn't different, it's going to be a **loser!**) Every competition has to have winners and losers, and the slogan approach is about the best way there is of sorting one from the other.

... and are the ideal tie-breaker

So you've got to become good at writing them!

For these reasons alone, slogan competitions are here to stay. And that means one thing. That any comper who wants to get in with the big prize-winners has got to become good at writing slogans. Not once or twice, when inspiration strikes - **every time**.

## But I'm no good at writing slogans!

You could be right!

And if, by the time you've read this manual and **seriously** tried out the methods it teaches, your slogan-writing hasn't improved then I'll have failed. Return it to the publishers in saleable condition within 30 days of receipt and ask for your money back. There'll be no quibbles.

To write good slogans ...

But I don't expect that to happen. The methods you're going to learn - **and see illustrated every step of the way by slogans that WERE winners** - are going to change all that. With them at your command you're going to be able to produce good slogans **every time**.

## But you can't teach me inspiration!

... you don't have to be inspired ...

I'm not going to try. For the simple reason that it's not needed! As Thomas Edison, the American inventor is famous for saying:

> *"Genius is one per cent inspiration and ninety-nine per cent perspiration."*

In other words, effort is what counts. You don't have to hope for a flash of blinding brilliance for that slogan you need. Not if you're prepared to put in a little bit of effort. With that, and the techniques you'll learn in this book, good slogans will just roll off the production line.

## I know what I want to say .. I'm just no good with words.

... or a great writer!

You don't have to be a Shakespeare to write good slogans! After all,

*Drinka Pinta Milka Day*

didn't exactly set the world of literature alight - but it certainly sold milk! And it wasn't a slogan that was invented by a slick advertising copy-writer. It was a 'bath-time' idea dreamed up by a man who worked for the Milk Marketing Board.

And as for:

> *Lipsmackin thirst quenchin (ace tastin motivatin good buzzin cool talkin high walkin fast livin ever givin cool fizzin) Pepsi ...*

You need **method**!

What more proof do you need? Besides which, most competition slogans only call for a dozen or so words anyway - and, as you'll discover, many of those words are pretty much chosen for you. The methods we'll be covering will provide the rest.

**You can't teach me anything. My slogans are always better than the ones that win! In fact, I can't understand why I don't win every time.**

Then maybe I can teach you something. For the simple reason that a lot of slogans don't win is, I suspect, **because they're losers to begin with**.

So that's where we're going to start. Because the first step in producing a slogan that's got a chance of winning is to avoid coming up with one that's virtually guaranteed to lose!

# 2

## Your slogan wasn't a winner because ...

Before you can win, you've got to make sure you're not a **loser**

... maybe it never had a chance?

Maybe it was a guaranteed loser. It's a hard fact to accept, but many slogans just don't have a chance to begin with.

Why? Here's why. The **5 DON'Ts** of slogan-writing. Avoid these obvious pitfalls, and you'll give your slogan a better chance of winning, simply by making sure that it won't have ruled itself out from the very start.

### DON'T use more than the number of words you're allowed.

Longer than allowed? It's a **loser.**

Every slogan competition gives clear instructions about how many words you're allowed to use.

*Complete in not more than* **X** *words*

it will say, where **X** will be anything from 8 to 20.

**Don't**, repeat **don't**, ignore this basic instruction. Obvious, I know, but it's all too easy to lose sight of this most basic of rules. And fatal. For the judges will have no alternative but to disqualify an over-long slogan. That's because competition results have to be published, by law. So the word limits have to be strictly applied. Let's face it, we'd all be pretty angry if they weren't - and what judge in his/her right mind would want to face a horde of furious entrants who did stick to the rules!

Winners are the right length ...

So, if you don't want your entry to go straight into the loser's pile, count carefully. In fact it's not a bad

... or shorter

idea to aim low in the first place. If you're allowed 12 words, then aim for using 10; if you're allowed 15, aim for 12; 20, then aim for 16. Assume that hyphenated words (like *economy-sized*) count as 2, but abbreviated words (like *I'd, I'm, it's* etc) count as 1. And count again before you finally send that slogan in.

**DON'T make it over-complicated.**

Take a tip from the classic slogans, those that have made millions, billions of pounds for their products.

For instance, would your imagination have been caught by a message like this?

Over-complicated? Then it's a **loser**.

> *Drink it at lunchtime, dinner time or in the evening .. it's truly international and sold all over the world .. and wherever you are, and whatever you're doing, it's great!*

Not a chance. That's why the classic was simplicity itself:

> *Martini. Any time, any place, anywhere.*

Think of any of the brilliant slogans from the past. (Whichever one comes to mind .. the fact that you **can** think of it - that it's stuck there in your mind - is a sure sign that it **was** a great slogan!). Now, try to whittle it down by even a single word. You'll find you can't do it.

Here's an example that's stuck with me:

> *A Mars a day helps you work, rest and play.*

Same thing again. Not a spare word in sight.

And a final one:

Winning slogans are **simple** slogans

> *Pick up a Penguin.*

How to say **everything** in four words!

That's the other test of a great slogan - try to think of an alternative way of conveying the same message as the original in **the same or fewer words**. Again, you'll find it's nearly impossible.

We'll come back to these classic slogans again, because they've got much more going for them than just simplicity. But for now that's the main lesson: **keep it simple**.

## DON'T use a slogan that sounds all wrong.

Sounds wrong? Then it's a **loser**

Fortunately, though it's tough to come up with a simple slogan, it's not hard to spot a complicated one. The acid test is: how does your slogan sound when you say it aloud? Try. That's what a judge will do, in his/her head if not actually out loud. Now, does it sound good? Does it 'roll off your tongue'? Because if it doesn't, then you've got to accept that it's almost certainly too complicated.

A winning slogan should just 'roll of the tongue'

On the previous page I quoted you the classic

*Pick up a Penguin*

as an example of an uncomplicated slogan. Well the other point to make about it is that it sounds good. It sticks in the mind. That's what a good slogan is supposed to do. And that's what you want to be sure your slogan's going to do - stick in the judge's mind.

So, make it sound good. If it doesn't, it's going to be a loser.

## DON'T use the first slogan that comes to mind.

Early thoughts are **losing** thoughts.

Why not?

Simple. Because if it was your first thought then you can be pretty sure it was the first thought that umpteen thousand other compers had as well.

It's vitally important to remember what was said earlier - the vast majority of competitions which ask for slogans are using them as **tie-breakers**; the judges

Winning ideas are different from everybody else's

simply can't pick a winner out of a thousand identical slogans! They've just **got** to pick something that's a bit different from the rest.

**How** do you make your slogan different? That's another question, and we'll be looking at it in plenty of detail later. What matters for now, is that you recognise the fact that writing a good slogan demands some effort. Not masses of effort - this manual isn't sub-titled ***the book that takes the 'slog' out of slogan-writing*** for nothing! - but more effort than simply jotting down the first thought that pops into your head. Just by doing that, you'll have taken the first step towards making your slogan different. In other words, towards ensuring that it's not a loser.

## DON'T ignore the rules.

"Rules are rules," goes the saying, and it applies to slogan competitions as well as any other area of life.

Rules are there to be obeyed - ignore them, and your slogan is a **loser**.

We've already mentioned the rule about slogan length. That's the most obvious one. But there are two other, less obvious but no less important, rules. Ignore them and you're a loser.

The first is buried in the same instruction that gives the maximum number of words you're allowed to use. You know the line ... it always seems to be the same:

> *Complete in not more than X apt and original words ...*

But that's the whole point. This rule is so very often the same that it's possible to miss the occasions when it's not. When, instead, it turns into:

> *Complete in not more than X apt, original and* ***amusing*** *words ...*

There's a pretty big difference between the two, and the best way I can illustrate it is with another couple of classic slogans. The first sold billions of bars of soap, and consisted of just two whispered initials:

*B. O.*

Winning slogans stick to the rules ...

Apt and original, I'm sure you'll agree, but not exactly amusing! It wasn't meant to be.

*It's what your right arm's for*

on the other hand, (excuse the pun!) sold beer by the barrel precisely because it was apt, original **and** amusing.

So remember, *apt and original* gives you a lot of scope. Basically, you can come up with anything. But if you're being asked for something *apt, original and humorous* then the options are narrowed down a lot. In the first case, your slogan can be warm, funny, serious ... the choice is yours. But in the second, it's just **got** to be amusing. That's what you're being asked for. Anything else, and it's into the losers pile. So follow the rules. If they're not the same as usual, then your slogan should be different too.

... and make sense!

The second easy-to-miss rule is that given by the **lead-in** ... that opening part of a sentence that your slogan is going to complete. We're going to come back time and time again to the lead-in, because it's vitally important. But the point I want to make here and now is that what you write - your slogan - has to follow the lead-in **and make sense**.

The whole thing, lead-in plus your slogan, has to hang together. Suppose, for example, you were entering a competition being run by the publishers of this book and the lead-in you were given was:

*I carry 'How To Write Competition Slogans' with me everywhere because ...*

We might decide that a good slogan would be something like:

*... it's worth its weight in gold*

Okay, it's not brilliant. It might not be a winner, but at least it makes sense. It's not a loser.

But what about something like:

> ... *I'm going far, so I'll say ta-ta!*

Well, it might be catchy but it doesn't actually have a lot to do with the subject of the lead-in. The whole sentence, lead-in plus slogan, has got to hang together. And

> *I carry 'How To Write Competition Slogans' with me everywhere because ...*
>
> ... *I'm going far so I'll say ta-ta!*

certainly does not! Another loser.

So, to summarise. Step number one in the quest for a winning slogan is to make sure that your entry isn't a loser to start with. That means you have to avoid the 5 DON'Ts of slogan writing:

**L onger than allowed**

**O ver-complicated**

**S ounds all wrong**

**E arly thought**

**R ules Ignored**

... because they spell LOSER.

# 3

## This slogan did win because ...

... it had something special about it.

In this chapter, we're going to take a number of slogans that did win prizes - some big prize-winners, some small - in a range of competitions. And we'll be looking at each of those slogans and asking the question that everyone who didn't win must have asked:

"Why did that slogan win? What did it have that mine didn't?"

Winning slogans follow a pattern ...

But we're going to do more than just look at winning slogans. We're going to **examine** them. We're going to look at those slogans for clues, clues that might give us some idea of why they were winners. In particular we'll be looking to see if those winning slogans had got anything in common.

Why? Because if there's a formula - and believe me, there is - then that's good to know. It means that all you have to do is follow that same formula to come up with winners of your own!

One more thing before we start this section.

... and the examples in this chapter were all **winners** ...

Apart from the couple of 'classic' slogans that are mentioned, every slogan we're going to look at was a winner of a recent competition - one that you may have entered. As it happens, they have all been selected from those listed in the *Winformation* section of the January 1990 issue of *Competitor's Companion.*

... and followed the same pattern ...

... a pattern that you can use - once you know what it is!

I've done this for two reasons:

1. So that you can check up on me if you want to! These are real winning examples.

2. So that you can see that what I'm going to teach you is generally applicable. I haven't scoured zillions of winning slogans looking for perfect examples of what I want to say. The lessons are there to see, month after month, in every slogan that wins.

So, away we go.

## Example No.1

House of Fraser, in combination with Le Creuset, ran a competition which offered as a prize a skiing holiday for two.

The lead-in was:

> *I have Le Creuset in my kitchen because ...*

The **winner** was an absolute beauty:

> *... there's snow risk of Le Creuset ever going downhill.*

So what was it about the winning slogan that must have caught the judge's eye? (Apart from the fact that it avoided the 5 DON'Ts of slogan-writing, of course!). I'll list a few things. You might think of others.

- ❑ It's got a good **message**: Le Creuset is all about **quality**.
- ❑ It mentions the **product** - Le Creuset.
- ❑ It refers to the **prize** (skiing) - not directly, but by cleverly using the skiing-related words ***snow*** and ***downhill***.
- ❑ It uses a couple of **word-plays** that are quite superb. ***Downhill*** clearly refers to the skiing prize, but it also use the adage, 'going downhill' meaning inferior. And the slogan is suggesting that it's quite impossible that such

inferiority could ever apply to Le Creuset. Thus, in a clever way, it's being very positive about **the product**.

- Finally there's another lovely word-play, using the prize-related word ***snow*** as a pun on the simple word ***no*** - a really neat way of getting another prize-related word into the slogan.

A cracking good slogan. But was it so very different to any of the other winners published at the same time?

## Example No.2

This was a competition promoted by Sunlight washing-up liquid, which offered the top prize of a Ford XR3i Cabriolet car, (or a cash alternative). The lead-in was:

> *Why does Sunlight washing-up liquid make washing up less of a chore ...*

and the winner announced as:

> *... Sunlight zooms through the dishes with the power and drive of a top performer.*

So, let's do the same thing again and try to put ourselves in the judge's shoes. What was it about this slogan that made it a winner?

- It's got a good **message**: that by using Sunlight the business of washing up is over and done with a lot quicker - which, as we'll see later, is just the message the lead-in was asking for.

- It mentions **the product** - Sunlight (notice how 'Sunlight' amounts to the same thing as saying 'Sunlight washing-up liquid' - except that it uses only one word instead of four!)

- ❑ It refers to **the prize** (sports car) by using the 'sporty' car-related words like ***power*** and ***drive***.

Never build your slogan on the cash alternative to the prize.

**Note**: unless the prize is cash, don't refer to it - even though you'd take it if you won. The car manufacturers could well be co-promoters of the competition, in which case they're likely to have a stake in the judging. And they're hardly going to pick a winning slogan which suggests that their prize isn't wanted!

- ❑ It uses **word-plays**, this time in the form of theme-links: that is, the use of words which manage to link two quite different subjects together. The word ***zoom*** conveys the impression of speed, and is used to link the image of a speedy car to that of a speedy washing-up liquid. The same effect is achieved through the use of the phrase ***top performer***, which suggests superiority over any other car/washing-up liquid around.

Are you beginning to see a pattern? One more, before we try to draw some points together.

## Example No.3

The Texas D-I-Y chain 'Solid Gold Winners' competition had as prizes £50,000-worth of solid gold ingots to be divided between 7 winners. For the competitor, the lead-in was just about as unhelpful as it is possible for a lead-in to be (why, you'll see later). It was:

*I like shopping at Texas because ...*

There were 7 winners. Let's just look at one of them.

*... With standards so high, Texas is the hallmark in DIY.*

Well, what was there about this slogan that made it a winner? By now, some of the points should be no surprise.

- It's got a clear **message** - you can expect quality in every way from Texas.

- It mentions the competition's **promoter** - Texas.

- It refers (indirectly) to **the prize** - gold. How?

- By means of **word-plays** in the form of theme-links, just as we saw in the Sunlight example. This time it was by using the words ***hallmark*** and ***standard***, both of which are related not only to gold, but to its quality. A nice example of killing two birds with one stone - the message was all about quality, remember.

- It mentions the **product** - DIY. Okay, so DIY isn't a product as such. That doesn't matter. If the lead-in is general, as this one was, then **the product is the sponsor** or the **sponsor's specialism**. In this case the sponsor's specialism was DIY - and that became the product.

- Finally, the slogan has further word-plays in the form of rhyme words, ***high*** and ***DIY***. Rhyme is very popular. It figures in many, many winning slogans. Why? Simple. Rhyme turns an ordinary slogan into something more catchy. To prove the point, turn the words of this one round a bit. *'With high standards, Texas is the hallmark in DIY'*. Still quite neat, because of the theme-links, but it hasn't got anything like the same impact. It doesn't 'sound' as good, does it?

## Is there a pattern?

Winning slogans have a clear message ...

and follow a clear referencing P- P- P- Policy ...

... Product

... Promoter

... Prize

... and they always use word-plays of some sort

Now, let's look back at those examples again. Three entirely different competitions, about entirely different products, and offering entirely different prizes. And yet the winning slogans have got so much in common about the way they've been put together:

- ❑ Each has a clear **message**, either taken from the lead-in, or one which suggests quality in general.
- ❑ Each has a direct mention of either the **product** or the competition's **promoter**; sometimes both.
- ❑ Each has a reference to the **prize** - either directly, or by using theme-link words.
- ❑ Each has **word-plays** of some sort. There are theme-links especially, and other types of word-plays such as the use of rhymes, but including other sorts of word plays like common sayings (adages) and puns.

Test these conclusions out on any winning slogans that you know of. See how they match up. It won't always be a perfect match - there's always the exception that proves the rule - but in the vast majority of cases, this is what you'll find:

- ❑ **Every winner** will have a **clear message about the product**. It will either be **taken from the lead-in** or, if the lead-in doesn't suggest one, **the message will be that the product is of high quality.**

**AND**

- ❑ **Every winner** will have at least one **word-play** of some sort, most often **relating to the product**

**AND**

- ❑ **Every winner** will refer to one or more of either the **product** OR the **promoter** OR the **prize** being offered.

Let's check this out against another winning example from that same January 1990 issue of *Competitor's Companion.*

## Example No.4

This was a competition co-promoted by Boots/Ambre Solaire, with the first prize of a Peugeot 205 Cabriolet car. The lead-in was:

> *Ambre Solaire offers the best protection because ...*

and the winner:

> *... Without sun burn and without pain I have that golden tan again*

Not a very strong slogan - but it's funny how often they win. Maybe it's because they follow the pattern. So, how do our conclusions match up?

It's got the two racing certainties:

- ❑ **Message**: straight from the lead-in - protection enables sun tan without pain.

- ❑ **Word-play**, in this case rhyme, with the words ***pain*** and ***again***; both relate to the product's qualities - namely, that it cuts out pain from sunbathing and it works every time.

And the winner comes up with the other racing certainty:

- ❑ A reference to one or more of **product/ promoter/prize**. In this example it's through product references, using the theme-link phrases ***sun burn*** and ***golden tan.***

Winning slogans fit a winning pattern.

So, where does all this get us? Simple. If you know what goes into a winning slogan, **you can make sure that your slogan fits that winning pattern.**

Which is not to say that you're going to win, of course. But it does mean that your slogan will certainly have all the qualities of a winner. And that's half the battle.

Okay, I hear you saying, so my slogan has got to have a clear message, and it's got to have word- plays of some sort.

But what message?

And I'm a disaster at English; I have enough trouble thinking of apt and original words, let alone making word-plays out of them. How do I come up with word-plays?

And how do I know whether it's best to mention the promoter or the product or the prize?

Help!!!!

Don't worry. All these questions are going to be answered in the next chapter. Some of them by me. But not too many. Because most of the answers are obvious. They stare you in the face every time you sit down to fill in your entry form.

**They are given to you!**

# 4

## Successful slogan-writing must begin with what you are given because ...

Everything you need to write a winning slogan is given to you ...

... what you're given tells you what the judges are going to be looking for!

So let's summarise. What exactly are you given in **every** competition? Four things:

- The competition **promoter**
- The **product** the competition is based on
- The **prize**
- The **lead-in**

and out of these, as we saw in the last chapter, you've got to come up with a slogan which has:

- a clear **message**
- some **word-plays**, ideally referring to the **product**
- mention of the **promoter**, the **product** or the **prize**.

Now, can you see the ways in which the two lists tie together?

... promoter

... product

- You're given the **promoter** - **ALWAYS.**
- You're given the **product** - **ALWAYS**. (Yes, even when the competition is about the promoter rather than any specific product. Because then the promoter **is** the product. If

the promoter is a supermarket chain, say, then that's what the product is - a supermarket.

... prize

- You're given the **prize** - **ALWAYS**.

So, what are you left to do? Firstly, find a clear **message**, and secondly a few **word-plays** to help put it across. And now I might surprise you:

Yes, and ...

... the message

- You're given the message - **ALWAYS!**

**AND**

... and everything you need for coming up with word-plays

- You're given the ammunition for making up more word-plays than you ever thought possible - **ALWAYS!**

## Not Getting The Message?

Well, you should. Without any trouble. Because that **message** is given to you **every** time. Where?

Your message comes from the lead-in ...

**It's in the lead-in.**

Every single lead-in will have a **message key- word** which points you towards the message that the judges are likely to be looking for. Spot that key-word, work on it - and the message your slogan must give will almost hit you in the eye!

... find the message key-word, and you've found your message.

To illustrate this, let's take another look at the examples we used in the previous chapter:

> *Why does Sunlight make washing-up less of a chore ...*

So, what's the message key-word in that lead-in? It shouldn't be hard to spot, not with only ten words to choose from! Strip away the words which are only there as padding (such as 'why') and you're only left with a couple to choose from:

- Sunlight/washing-up (they amount to the same thing)

- Chore

Remove the padding words (*why, of, or* etc) from the lead-in and what you're left with are the possible message key-words.

Usually there'll be only one that's worth considering.

Here's a simple rule: the message key-word is only the product if no other key-words are possible. That's not the case here. The message key-word is **chore.**

Now, what is a chore? Something that's tiresome and boring. But washing-up is unavoidable (if you haven't got a dishwasher - and you wouldn't be using Sunlight if you had!) so what's the only thing that can make it less of a chore? Speed. Having identified chore as the key-word, that's got to be the message.

And what was the winner? A slogan that had a message that was all about speed:

> *... Sunlight zooms through the dishes with the power and speed of a top performer.*

Here's another winner we looked at:

> *Ambre Solaire offers the best protection because ...*

So, what's the message key-word in that lead-in? There's only one choice: **Protection**! Protection from the sun. Take it further. Without protection from the sun you're going to suffer the pain of sunburn.

So the message can only be about one thing - that the product helps prevent the pain of sunburn. Which was just the message the winning slogan came across with:

> *... Without sun burn and without pain I have that golden tan again.*

The other two examples weren't so clear-cut though. If you remember, the lead-ins were much more general. There was:

> *I have Le Creuset in my kitchen because ..*

and one which I described as being just about as unhelpful as it's possible for a lead-in to be:

> *I shop at Texas because ...*

Where are the key-words in those two lead-ins? Well,

the first only leaves you with two choices - **kitchen** or **Le Creuset**. In the second, you've only got one choice: **Texas**.

The product or promoter must be the message key-word if no other alternatives exist.

So how can **Texas** or **Le Creuset** be a message key-word? Because they are the product the competition's all about. Unlike the character Michelle in *'Allo 'Allo* I am saying this more than once! If the competition isn't about a specific product then **the competition promoter must be treated as the product.**

If the message key-word is the product/ promoter, then the message is about **quality**

So what's the message going to be in such cases? Simple. It's going to be about **quality** - the quality of service offered by the competition's promoter. This means your slogan will either be one which suggests that the promoter offers unbeatable quality in general, or one which talks about a particular quality.

So:

> *... There's snow chance of Le Creuset ever going downhill*

gives a message about **quality in general**.

And

> *... With standards so high, Texas is the hallmark in DIY*

gives a message about a **particular quality area** - DIY - of the promoter's product or specialism.

In that competition, promoted by Texas, there were another six winners of £7,000 worth of gold ingots besides the one I've been using as an example. Look at those other six winners:

> *... The hallmark of price and quality makes Texas a DIY goldmine*
>
> *... For minor repairs or major renovation - they offer value, choice and motivation!*
>
> *... When value is the question - Texas is the answer.*

*... Winning gold by saving pence - that's good old Texan common sense.*

*... Going for gold by saving pence really does make homecare sense.*

*... For service and friendly smiles, Texas beats the rest by miles.*

What are they all talking about? **Quality!**

The three main **qualities** areas are ...

There are variations, of course, but in the end you'll find that these types of slogan boil down to a message on the quality of the product/promoter in one of only a very limited number of specific topic areas. Just **three,** in fact:

... good value

... good choice

... good service

- ❑ quality - you get value for money
- ❑ quality - you get a wide choice
- ❑ quality - you get a good service

So, if the key-word from the lead-in ends up being the promoter, then your **message will be about quality**. If the promoter specialises in a particular area - DIY or whatever - then pick on the quality of that specialism and bring it into your slogan.

Either angle your message at overall quality, or one of the 3 'qualities' mentioned above - and away you go!

## Playing With Words

So you've got your message. You know **what** you want to say.

The only problem left now is: **how** do you say it in a way that will catch the judge's attention? Where do the essential word-plays come from, I expect you're saying? We're certainly not given them!

That's true. But let me surprise you again. You are only half right.

Sure, you've got to come up with the word-plays yourself - although in the next chapter we'll see how even that can be turned into an exercise that can't fail.

Word-plays emerge from key-words that are given to you ...

But you're wrong if you think that you're given nothing. You most certainly are. Word-plays don't have to be plucked out of thin air. They simply have to build on starting points that are there waiting for you to use. They are **given** to you.

It's all down to spotting **key-words** again. This time, though, it's a case of looking for key-words which are the starting point, not for the message that you're going to convey - we've dealt with that already - but for the **theme** of your slogan.

To illustrate this point, let's look at a different example to those we've used so far. (But still one that was listed in the January 1990 issue of *Competitor's Companion*).

This was a competition promoted by Robinson's, the fruit drink people. The prizes weren't mind-boggling - limited editions of a Robinsons model lorry!

... usually by the lead-in ...

But the interesting thing about this particular competition was the number of winning slogans - 250 of them! Every one different in some way, and all from the simple lead-in:

*Robinson's keep you on the road because ..*

I'm not planning to study all 250 winners! Here's just a small sample:

*... It's the perfect 'break' fluid!*

*... The juice in the bottle gives you more at the throttle*

*... Even the traffic lights show Robinson's orange*

*... A Robinson's reviver is great for every driver*

*... You get more smiles to the gallon with Robinson's*

*... It has the winning formula to squash any thirst*

*... It's a million times better than a jug-a-nought!*

Now, what do they all have in common?

Answer: they're all using word-plays that have built in some way on either the key-word ***road*** which was given in the lead-in, or the prize ***lorry***. Taken together, they give the clear theme for the required slogan: **motoring.**

... in the form of **theme-words.**

The starting point for your slogan, then, is to come up with a list of slogan key-words which identify one (sometimes it's more) **theme-words** for your slogan. The **theme-word(s)** are always there. And they have to be used. They're vitally important. They're the building blocks for your word-plays.

Where do the themes come from? Well, you won't have far to look. Usually, no further than the lead-in.

Sometimes the theme is connected with the prize ...

The easiest slogans to write are those that have a lead-in like that in the Robinsons competition we've just been looking at. That was an example of a lead-in giving you the clearest indication of a theme. Given the combination of ***road*** from the lead-in and the ***lorry*** prize, there couldn't have been too much doubt about working with an overall theme-word of ***motoring***.

The Ambre Solaire competition was even more obvious:

*Ambre Solaire offers the best protection because ...*

... sometimes with the product ...

is a lead-in that refers to the product; nothing more, nothing less. There's no theme-link suggested, such as that in the Robinson's example we've just looked at. Here, the theme-word can only be **the product itself** - meaning that any word-plays for this slogan will be built on the theme-word **sun** ... of which **suntan,**

**sunburn** etc. are the most obvious of examples. The winner:

> ... *Without sun burn and without pain I have that golden tan again.*

did just that.

Some lead-ins, however, will have more than one possibility for a theme-word. This is where it can start to get tricky!

Here's another winning example, this time from a competition jointly promoted by Tesco and the drinks people, Schweppes. The lead-in was:

> *Straight Schweppes tonic is the perfect straight drink because ...*

... and sometimes with a particular quality that the product claims to have.

Here, the obvious theme-word is ***drink*** (of which ***tonic*** is the example that must be used). But it's also got the word ***perfect*** - could that be used as the basis for a general theme-word, ***quality***? The answer is, yes. There can be more than one theme -word. Sometimes you can be given too much!

In this case the winning slogan was:

> ... *Lots to drink at Tesco's price, ice cold tonic with lemon slice*

which had a word-play on the drink-related word ***slice***, and based its message on the message key-word ***perfect.***

Not all lead-ins give as much.

> *I have Le Creuset in my kitchen because ...*

gave only ***kitchen*** as a possibility, and the winner didn't use it.

> ... *There's snow chance of Le Creuset ever going downhill*

built on another source of slogan theme-words: **the prize**.

The first steps in creating word-plays are ..

So, what are the main sources of slogan theme- words. They are, in order of likely importance:

- the lead-in
- the product
- the prize

... find a **main theme-word** (which **must** be related to your slogan's message key-word ...

Take them in this order and aim for two theme-words. Three at the most. These are going to generate word-plays, remember, and more than three theme-words will be quite unmanageable.

And one of them **must,** repeat **must,** be related to the key-word that you've used as the basis of your message. That means it must come from the lead-in, whether it's a clearly stated word or the theme-word **quality** (in cases where the lead-in is one of the general *I shop at X's because* ... type.

... and a maximum of two other (secondary) theme-words.

And that's it. Two simple methods to enable you to find out, from the information you're actually given,

- the key-word for your message
- two theme-words on which to build some word-plays for your slogan.

All that's left now is to produce a slogan using word-plays that are apt and original!

Ah, you might be thinking. The impossible bit.

No good with words?

Flunked English every time?

Don't worry. We've a technique for coming up with apt and original words as well. A **power** technique that will generate word-plays by the dozen. A technique known as **Brainstorming**.

## 5

# You <u>can</u> complete whatever sentence you're given in an apt and original way because ...

Word-plays don't have to be the result of great talent! They can be **manufactured** ...

... the apt and original words you're going to need are all going to be related to the theme- words you've already found. That being the case, what you need is a technique that starts from those words and uses them to come up with a whole host of word-plays - because, remember: every winning slogan has at least one word-play in it.

That's where the technique of **Brainstorming** comes in.

... and the first step in the process is **brainstorming** ...

It's a technique used by all manner of creative people, from top advertising teams through to top managers in industry, from top song-writers in search of inspiration through to top comedy writers looking for new jokes. Why? Because **Brainstorming generates ideas.**

You might have heard of the word before. It's sometimes used to excuse somebody who's done something completely out of character - you know, like a vicar swearing, or a traffic warden smiling! We say "Oh, he/she must have had a brainstorm." In other words, we're saying that they must have done whatever it was without thinking.

Well, believe it or not, that really is what brainstorming is about! About doing something without thinking!

We're going to take our main theme-word and brainstorm around it, writing down absolutely anything at all that comes to mind. Anything and everything, without any thought of whether or not it will be of use in a slogan. And the most important thing about this step is that it's the sort you've always dreamed about - you know, the exercise you can do without thinking? Well, that's the case here.

More than that, in fact. **You're not allowed to think!**

... which involves taking your main theme-word and writing down any related words ...

That's absolutely essential. You will be thinking (that is, being critical) later. But not now.

That's because the brainstorming technique has two phases to it. This is the first phase, and it involves completely switching off the 'thinking' part of the brain. (You might be one of those people who would say this will be no trouble at all! In which case, be prepared for a surprise. Not thinking is harder than you think!)

**... without thinking!!**

With brainstorming phase 1 then, you're going to write down anything that comes to mind. The critical part, the 'thinking' part comes later, so you can feel perfectly free to just let your imagination go where it wants.

To illustrate what happens, let's take a realistic example from scratch. Imagine that the publishers of this book are running a competition.

Here's an example ... starting from scratch.

The first prize is terrific: an all-expenses paid trip to Florida for two to see the launching of the next space shuttle mission from Cape Kennedy! All you have to do is complete in not more than 15 apt and original words:

> *I think 'How To Write Competition Slogans' is a manual that's out of this world because ...*

Now, let's follow step-by-step through each of the techniques that we've been talking about in this book so far.

1. Find the message key-word ...

**Step 1: What has the slogan's message got to be?**

**Q:** Is there a message key-word in the lead-in?

**A:** No, there isn't. Not directly. The phrase ***out of this world*** is just another way of saying ***great*** or ***terrific*** . So, that tells us that:

- THE MESSAGE KEY-WORD IS: **THE PRODUCT**

So our slogan message is going to be about some aspect of the product's quality.

... and from this, what the slogan's message is going to be.

**Q:** Does the product specialise?

**A:** Yes. It's a book, so it must specialise. In this case, the specialism is in 'How To Write Competition Slogans'.

So (just as a slogan about a DIY store would concentrate on that specialism) our slogan is going to concentrate on the **quality** of the specialist area of the book: competition slogan-writing. Our message is going to be:

- THE PRODUCT HELPS YOU WRITE GOOD COMPETITION SLOGANS

2. Then, as a source of word-plays, find the main theme-word ...

**Step 2: What is the main theme-word our slogan's word plays are going to come from?**

**Q:** Is there a theme-word suggested by the lead-in?

**A:** Yes. The lead-in has a clear link to a theme through its use of the phrase ***out of this world***.

This suggests the theme-word:

- SPACE

**Q:** Does this word check against either the product or the prize?

**A:** Yes. Space-travel has nothing to do with the product, but everything to do with the prize.

So the main slogan key-word is: SPACE

... and

3. another one or two secondary theme-words.

### Step 3: What other slogan theme-words are there?

Checking in order:

- the **lead-in** ... gives us two possibles from the title of the book: SLOGAN-WRITING is one, and COMPETITION is the other.
- the **product** ... specialises in competition slogan-writing. This confirms the suggestions made by inspecting the lead-in.
- the **prize** ... is about space-travel. This confirms the main theme word suggested by the lead-in.

So we have three theme-words to use for the basis of a brainstorm:

**SPACE** - the main theme-word

**SLOGAN-WRITING** - the second theme-word

**COMPETITION** - the third theme-word

Now we're ready to **brainstorm!**

That's the first part of the exercise completed. We know what our message is going to be, and we know the theme-words that are going to form the basis of our word plays.

Now it's time to switch off the thinking part of the brain and just let it roam!

4. Using the main theme-word ...

## Step 4: Brainstorm on the main slogan key-word.

We take the main theme-word first. Forget the other two for now. That is, we're going to write down anything that comes into mind in any way connected with **SPACE**.

At this point let me make a suggestion. To prove to yourself how powerful this technique is, don't read any further for now. Spend just **five minutes** coming up with a Brainstorm list of your own. That way you can work with your list and see for yourself just how many slogans you can come up with for yourself. You'll be amazed!

write down as many **related** words or phrases as you can.

Here's the list I came up with in **three minutes**:

| | | |
|---|---|---|
| star | planet | moon |
| sun | rocket | blast-off |
| shuttle | launch-pad | stratosphere |
| orbit | countdown | splashdown |
| Earth | Mars | Saturn |
| Mercury | Jupiter | Neptune |
| Pluto | Uranus | moon |
| space | outer-space | spaceman |
| spacewalk | comet | astronaut |
| cosmonaut | cosmos | light-year |
| landing | mission control | |
| sputnik | satellite | booster rocket |
| lunar module | skylab | universe |
| galaxy | Star Trek | Star Wars |
| E.T. | alien | Big Bang |
| Milky Way | | |

If you thought of more, or different words, then that's a great sign. It means that, in a real competition, you and I would have been likely to produce different slogans. And if we're different then we're **not so likely to be losers**!

As I suggested before, now follow through the rest of this example using your own brainstorm words. It's going to be a revelation for you!

5. Then, for each word in your brainstorm list, come up with any ...

## Step 5: TAP the Table.

The next step inolves using the brainstorm words we've just produced.

What happens, basically, is that we brainstorm again - but, this time, by building on the words we've already got. The aim of this step is to build up a collection of word-plays. Again though, remember the golden rule for brainstorming - **leave the thinking until later!** Don't worry about whether a word or phrase seems at all useful. We'll be making that decision all in good time.

So, what are we aiming at? Three things:

- ❑ Tie-words

... Tie-words (i.e. alternative meanings) ...

A tie-word is going to be any alternative meaning that the brainstorm word can have. For instance, ***star*** refers to the twinkly things in the sky at night, but it is also used in another way - as a word to describe a person, or object even, that's outstanding in some way.

- ❑ Adages

... Adages (i.e. well-known phrases or sayings) ... ...

Adages are well-known sayings. We're looking for anything well-known, perhaps an old saying, a proverb, a TV catch-phrase - anything that's related in some way to the brainstorm word and which would be instantly recognised by the vast majority of people.

- ❑ Puns

... Puns (similar-sounding words or phrases)

A pun is a simply any word that sounds like the brainstorm word. It doesn't matter whether it's related or not, since the object of using a pun is to refer to the original word in a funny way.

It's corny, I know, but you can remind yourself that you're looking for Tie-ins, Adages and Puns by taking their initial letters and remembering that in this step you **TAP the Table**.

Set the results out in an easy-to-read way - a table is best.

Below you'll see our original brainstorm words laid out in a table. Each word gets a row of its own, and against it there can be up to three entries in each of the TAP columns. Don't expect every brainstorm word to have something in each column. They won't.

| **Brainstorm** | **Tie-word** | **Adage** | **Pun** |
|---|---|---|---|
| star | famous | star-studded<br>film star<br>starlit night | |
| planet | | | plan it |
| moon | go all sloppy | man in the moon<br>once in a blue moon<br>cow jumped over the moon | |
| sun | | sunshine | son |
| rocket | go fast | | rock it |
| | firework | | |
| blast-off | take off | | |
| shuttle | shuttlecock | | |
| launchpad | | | |
| stratosphere | | | |
| orbit | | go into orbit | |
| countdown | get closer | | |
| splashdown | | | |
| Earth | | Mother Earth<br>what on earth?<br>down to earth | |
| Mars | spoils | | |
| | chocolate bar | work, rest and play | |
| Saturn | | | sat on |
| Mercury | thermometer | the mercury's rising | |
| Jupiter | | | |
| Neptune | sea-king | | |
| Pluto | cartoon character | | |
| Uranus | | | (no! we can't use that one!) |
| space | open space | outer-space<br>stare into space | outa space |
| spaceman | | | space, man |

| Brainstorm | Tie-word | Adage | Pun |
|---|---|---|---|
| spacewalk | | | |
| comet | | Halley's comet | don't come it |
| astronaut | | | astro-nought |
| cosmonaut | | | cosmo-nought |
| cosmos | | | |
| light-year | long time | | |
| landing | top of stairs | | |
| mission | job, task | | |
| mis'n control | | | |
| sputnik | | | |
| satellite | | | set alight |
| booster | give a lot of help | | |
| lunar module | | | |
| skylab | | | |
| universe | | | |
| galaxy | | | |
| Star Trek | | Mr Spock<br>Captain Kirk<br>boldly go where no man has gone before | |
| Star Wars | | C3PO<br>R2D2 | |
| E.T. | | | |
| alien | | space invader | |
| Big Bang | explosion | | |
| Milky Way | | | |

6. Now brainstorm with the secondary theme-words

## Step 6: Brainstorm the Table with the secondary slogan theme-words

Now we go through the table again. Again we take every brainstorm word, but this time we're looking for tie-ins with either of our secondary slogan key-words, 'slogan-writing' and 'competition'. Don't worry if you don't spot many. Most of our slogans are going to come from what we've got already from brainstorming the primary word.

The revised table I came up with is laid out on this page and the next. The additions to it as a result of brainstorming on our secondary theme- words ***slogan-writing*** and ***competition*** are printed in bold type. ***(sw)*** means that it came from the ***slogan-writing*** theme-word, (c) from brainstorming on the theme-word ***competition*** .

| Brainstorm | Tie-word | Adage | Pun |
|---|---|---|---|
| star | famous<br>**the best (c)** | star-studded<br>film star<br>starlit night | |
| planet | | | plan it |
| moon | go all sloppy<br>**top prize (c)** | man in the moon<br>**shoot for the moon(c)**<br>once in a blue moon<br>cow jumped over the moon | |
| sun | | sunshine | son |
| rocket | go fast<br>firework | | rock it |
| blast-off | take off | | |
| shuttle | shuttlecock | | |
| launchpad | **writing pad (sw)** | | |
| stratosphere | | | |
| orbit | | go into orbit | |
| countdown | get closer | | |
| splashdown | | | |
| Earth | **thinking hard (sw)** | Mother Earth<br>what on earth?<br>down to earth | |
| Mars | spoils<br>chocolate bar | work, rest and play | |
| Saturn | | | sat on |
| Mercury | thermometer | the mercury's rising | |
| Jupiter | | | |
| Neptune | sea-king | | **seeking (sw)** |
| Pluto | cartoon character | | |
| Uranus | | | (no! we can't use that one!) |

| **Brainstorm** | **Tie-word** | **Adage** | **Pun** |
|---|---|---|---|
| space | open space<br>**no ideas (sw)** | outer-space<br>stare into space | outa space |
| spaceman | | | space, man |
| spacewalk | | | |
| comet | | Halley's comet | don't come it |
| astronaut | | | astro-nought |
| cosmonaut | | | cosmo-nought |
| cosmos | | | |
| light-year | long time<br>**wait for idea(sw)** | | |
| landing | top of stairs | | |
| mission | job, task | | |
| mis'n control | **message (sw)** | | |
| sputnik | | | |
| satellite | | | set alight |
| booster | give a lot of help<br>**help win (c)** | | |
| lunar module | | | |
| skylab | | | |
| universe | | | **uni-verse(sw)** |
| galaxy | | | |
| Star Trek | **journey to a star(sw)**<br>**slogan (sw)** | Mr Spock<br>Captain Kirk<br>boldly go where no man has gone before | |
| Star Wars | | C3PO<br>R2D2 | |
| E.T. | | | |
| alien | | space invader | |
| Big Bang | explosion | | |
| Milky Way | | | |

Again, you could well have thought of many more than I have. The longer you spend on this part, the more words you'll come up with - and the more slogans you'll generate. How? By using the table you've built up. the table above is going to produce 20 good slogans for us. And **every table you construct will do the same!**

# 6

## You have plenty of slogan ideas and word-plays now, because ...

... they're all sitting there in the brainstorm table you've just constructed, just waiting to jump out!

This is where you start to see the power of the brainstorming method come into play. (As you become more experienced you'll find you're spotting the slogan possibilities as you're building up the table).

With your slogan message and the lead-in in mind ...

Turn the brain on again! Now work line-by line through the table, with both your message and the lead-in in mind. You might find it helps to actually write both down on a separate sheet of paper and have them beside you as you do this step.

... work line-by-line through your table ...

Now, every time an entry in the table triggers a thought for a likely slogan, write it down. Do this quickly. Don't get sidetracked into worrying about word counts or finding rhymes at this stage. Just take the idea and write it down in as many words as you need to convey that slogan message.

... and write down any slogan ideas that you can see from what's in the table.

Let's carry on with our example to see how this stage works out. Remember, our slogan message - generated in Step 1 - is:

> *THE PRODUCT (THIS BOOK) HELPS YOU WRITE GOOD COMPETITION SLOGANS*

and the lead-in:

> *I think 'How To Write Competition Slogans' is a manual that's out of this world because ...*

You will find there's plenty there ...

So, here's my starter list (again, do this exercise with your own words and compare results) taken from the different entries in the brainstorm table - which draft slogan comes from which entry should be pretty obvious. I came up with no less than 14:

- ❑ ... It helps turn dull slogans into stars!
- ❑ ... When slogan-writing's the mission - it helps me 'planet'!
- ❑ ... Now I can come up with good slogans every time, not just once in a blue moon
- ❑ ... It helps my slogans take-off
- ❑ ... It turns my writing pad into a launchpad for good slogans
- ❑ ... It helps send my slogans into orbit
- ❑ ... It means I no longer think 'what on earth can I write?'
- ❑ ... I spend less time Saturn my backside!
- ❑ ... It stops me staring into space, man!
- ❑ ... It gives me lots of star ideas, not astro-nought!
- ❑ ... It means the ideas don't take light-years to arrive
- ❑ ... It helps my slogans boldly go where no man has gone before
- ❑ ... It's the slogan-writers' equivalent of the Big Bang

That's 14 pretty good slogans!

... and they'll **automatically** fit winning pattern the judges tend to look for!

All of them automatically match the profile of a winning slogan - the sort that a judge would automatically be looking for - because they've been produced using the information supplied by the product, the prize and the lead-in.

But at the moment they're only in rough form.

What's needed is one final step. To put them into winning shape by making them 'sound' right.

And that's all down to technique as well!

# 7

# And you can make your slogans 'sound' right because ...

A 'right-sounding' slogan comes from ...

... it all comes down to key-words and a simple technique yet again!

What you need to do now is to work on every one of those rough draft slogans to make them as catchy as possible. And, as you saw when we looked at what makes a winning slogan, that so often means some sort of rhyme.

... polishing those word-plays ...

Okay, so you were hopeless at poetry at school! But what's needed here is nothing terribly complicated. You don't need to be a Wordsworth or a Byron. More of a Pam Ayres, in fact.

What I mean by that is that you need only to find some simple rhymes - nothing fantastically poetical at all. And that's something anyone is able to do.

But rhymes to what? Let's take the first of our 'out of this world' draft slogans and see. This is it:

- ❑ ... It helps turn dull slogans into stars

... and a winning way is by using rhyme.

Now remember, using a rhyme is a way, not only of making a slogan sound better, but of adding **emphasis** to a particular word. So it makes sense to choose the word that you're aiming to rhyme with very carefully - because you're effectively going to be 'sounding' that word twice.

Rhymes should focus attention on the main slogan theme-word.

So, what's always likely to be the best word to go for? The **main slogan theme-word**, of course! The theme-word from your brainstorm which triggered the whole rough slogan in the first place!

That means, in this example, that the word we're going to emphasise - the word we're going to generate a rhyme for - is the theme-word ***stars.***

The technique now is simple. Write down every word you can think of that rhymes with ***stars.*** But not at random - that's the hard way of doing anything. Use a method.

Rhyme words are easy to produce ...

Rub out the prefix of the word you're tring to rhyme with (that is, 'st' in the case of star). Then try alternative possible start letters, simply by running your way through the alphabet

... so long as you use a **method**!

So, in searching for rhymes with ***stars*** ...

'a' gives us nothing

'b' gives us ***bars***

'c' gives ***cars*** and so on.

Try each of the possibilities in turn. Don't forget to try the compound starters, like 'br' and 'cr'. The table on the next page gives a check-list you can work from.

And, most importantly, don't worry if the rhyme words seem hopeless. You're only looking for one, remember. If you find any more than that then you've got a bonus.

And don't worry about whether the rhyme word is any use. This is brainstorming in rhyme - the thinking comes later!

So, what have we got to rhyme with ***star***?

bars/ bras/ cars/ chars/ jars/ Mars/ pars/ scars/ spars

And there's the one: Mars! It's doubly good, because it both means to make faulty, and it's the name of a planet - a theme-link to our key-word! (It's also in our brainstorm table, so we'd have got to it later anyway).

So we work on our draft slogan with the aim of rhyming stars with Mars - and we end up with: something like:

> *... It neither hinders nor Mars - but makes dull slogans stars!*

Get the idea? To summarise, then. The three step method to producing a rhyming slogan from your draft slogan is:

- ❑ Find your main slogan theme-word
- ❑ List all possible rhyme words for that theme-word
- ❑ Pick the best of the rhyme words (there may be more than one!) and rework your draft slogan to use it.

**Rhyme-Words Prefix Checklist**

A-
B- BL- BR-
C- CH- CL- CR-
D- DR-
E-
F- FL- FR-
G- GL- GR-
H-
I-
J-
K- KR-
L-
M-
N-
O-
P- PH- PL- PR-
QU-
R-
S- SC- SH- SHR- SK- SL- SM- SN-
SP- SQU- ST- SW-
T- TH- TR- TW-
U-
V-
W-
X-
Y-

Let's take another one of our draft slogans to see those steps in action again.

> *(I think 'How To Write Competition Slogans' is out of this world because ...)*
>
> *... When slogan- writing's the mission - it helps me 'planet'!*

What's the key-word? In this case, ***Planet*** - a punning word-play which we're using to suggest the phrase ***plan it.***

So when we list the rhyme words this time, it's to look for a rhyme with ***plan it***.

Running through the list of possible alternative starting characters we get our rhyme-words:

ban it/ can it?/ fan it/ man it/ pan it/ ran it/ scan it/ span it/ tan it/ than it/ van it

Now, a word of caution. **Do not gild the lily!**

If you've got a good word-play already - such as ***planet*** for ***plan it*** in this case - adding a rhyme can actually weaken its effect; in other words, a rhyme can actually count against you by making your slogan LESS effective.

Remember the 2nd in our 5 DON'Ts of slogan-writing: DON'T make it complicated! So, be very sure that any additional word-play such as a rhyme will actually add something to what you've already got.

**But don't use rhyme for the sake of it! It might reduce the affect of a good word-play. So ...**

With the rhyme-words we've generated for this example, I think that's the case. None of them really stand out. The only possible, strangely enough, is the simplest - 'than it'. It could be used to give:

> *... there's no better book than it, to help writers 'planet'.*

But, personally, I don't think this is as good as the non-rhyming original. Try as I might, for instance, I couldn't get my secondary theme-word ***slogan*** to fit into it easily. So, on balance, I'd stick with the original

> *... When slogan- writing's the mission - it helps me 'planet'!*

**... Be critical!**

You may not agree; you may have a slogan that is similar, but a lot better! The important point here is: be critical. If you've got a really strong word-play, take care about adding a rhyme. My rule would be: if in doubt, leave it out.

Those two examples we've just looked at cover both sides of the coin: when to use a rhyme, and when not. But notice what I promised you right at the start of this manual: you've no longer got the problem of worrying about where a decent slogan is going to come from. Quite the opposite - you're worrying about which ones to throw away! And that's a much nicer problem, I'm sure you agree!

So, using the same technique, let's look at every one of the remaining 12 draft slogans to see how they work out. We'll look at each in the same critical way, to see how best to make it into the sort of slogan that might catch a judge's eye.

**Original:**

*Now I can come up with good slogans every time, not just once in a blue moon*

The **main slogan theme-word** is: ***moon***

This gives us **rhyme-words:**

boon/ balloon/ croon/ dune/ goon/ hewn/ june/ noon/ rune/ soon/ spoon/ swoon/ tune

Don't be surprised if your search for rhyme words actually generates even more ideas for slogans!

There are some good possibilities here. And this is something that you'll often find - searching for rhyme words will actually increase your number of slogans. We can get two good ones from this list, for instance:

*... you can shoot for the moon with this slogan-writer's boon*

*... it makes ideas come soon - not once in a blue moon!*

*

**Original:**

*It helps my slogans take-off*

The **main slogan theme-word(s)** are: ***take (off)***

This time, though, we are limited in our choice of **rhyme-words;** any we go for must be capable of having the word ***off*** tacked on the end. This gives us only:

brake-off/ flake-off/ rake-off/ shake-off

Not much, but good enough to give us another couple of rhyming versions!

*... it helps take the brake off, and my slogans take off!*

*... my slogans take off, and the prizes I rake off!*

**Original:**

*... It turns my writing pad into a launch-pad for good slogans*

The **main slogan theme-word** is: ***pad*** - a source of a great number of rhyme words.

BUT!!

If you've got a good word-play, it's often better to rework it instead of forcing in a rhyme.

And besides ...

This one already has a word-play that can hardly be bettered. ***Launch-pad*** and ***writing-pad*** go brilliantly together. They combine the lead-in, the product AND the prize! What more could you want? I would say work on what's there, rather than spoil it by forcing in a rhyme. So I've done nothing more than rework it slightly into:

*... It turns my writing-pad into a slogan launch-pad.*

*

**Original:**

*... It helps send my slogans into orbit*

The **main slogan theme-word** is: ***orbit***

... sometimes there just isn't a rhyme there ...

This gives us **rhyme-words** of ... embarassingly, none at all. You may do better, but I couldn't think of any at all. So, what now?

Simple. Either we throw this one out - there's plenty more where it came from, remember - or we work on it some more.

... in which case, try some more theme-links.

If we're going to work on it, then the best way is to add in some more theme-links. Scan the brainstorm list again for some ideas. There'll be plenty there. For instance, we could use ***launch*** instead of send. We could also bring in the idea of winning the prize and end up with:

*... it helps launch my slogans into a prize-winning orbit!*

**Original**:

*... It means I no longer think 'what on earth can I write?'*

The **main slogan theme-word** is: ***earth***

Again, with this draft slogan we've got a good word-play on the theme of space travel. It might be improved by a rhyme, it might not.

As you gain experience, you'll be able to spot those that can and those that can't. You'll also be able to spot - and this is a perfect example - those draft slogans that need another theme-link rather than a rhyme.

A good way of adding another theme-link is by looking to see if two of your draft slogans would be better combined.

When that happens, try combining two of your draft slogans to see where that gets you. I was prompted to do that in this case because my eye spotted the next draft slogan in the list:

*... I spend less time Saturn my backside*

That's got another neat theme-link, but again it perhaps doesn't say as much as it could. Put the two together though, and they give a really good 'sitting and thinking' slogan:

*(I think 'How To Write Competition Slogans is out of this world because ...)*

*... I'm no longer Saturn my backside thinking 'what on earth can I write?'!*

*

**Original**:

*... I write slogans instead of staring into space*

The **main slogan theme-word** is: ***space***

This gives us **rhyme-words**:

ace/ brace/ case/ chase/ face/ grace/ lace/ mace/ pace/ place

The word 'pace' is an obvious pointer to a slogan which fits in with our slogan message - that the product (this book) HELPS with the task of slogan-writing. Speed and efficiency are standard ways in which a product can help, and ***pace*** is suggestive of both. So we could have:

> *... Now I don't stare into space 'cos ideas come on apace!*

Don't just work on the rhyme - work on the 'beat' of the slogan as well. It's got to sound right.

The reason for using ***apace*** rather than ***pace***, and ***'cos*** instead of ***because*** is simple: they give us a slogan that sounds better. Remember DON'T no. 3 - Sounds All Wrong? So, work with your main theme-word and its rhyme words until you've got a slogan that trips off the tongue.

Another slogan from the same set of theme-words could be:

> *... Now I write hip slogans instead of staring into space, man*

This one has combined two brainstorm words, ***space*** and ***spaceman*** in an original way. Adding ***hip*** as an adjective to slogans gives another "beatnik" touch. It's stretching the theme-link quite a lot, but this is worth a try once in a while - especially if you're submitting multiple entries.

*

**Original**:

> *... It gives me lots of star ideas, not astro-nought!*

With this one, I'd again argue that the word-play with ***astro-nought*** is so strong that to add a rhyme would be to lessen its impact. But, as I'm trying to give you as many examples as possible, let's push this one a bit further.

The **main slogan theme-word** is: ***astronaut***

This gives a decent list of **rhyme-words**:

bought/ brought/ caught/ fought/ fraught/ quart/ sort/ short/ snort/ sport/ taut/ taught/ thought/ wrought

So, how about ...

> ... *More slogans per thought - all stars, not astro-nought!*

Or ...

> ... *Slogans, long and short - dozens, not astro-nought!*

Or

> ... *With the techniques we're taught come endless slogans, not astro-nought!*

Personally, I still prefer the non-rhyming version.

*

**Original:**

> ... *It means the ideas don't take a light-year to arrive*

The **main slogan theme-word** is: ***light-year***

A double-rhyme can be produced using exactly the same method ...

We have a different problem for rhyming here. Going for a rhyme on ***year*** would be simple enough. But think a little more. Wouldn't it be even more effective to come up with a 'double rhyme' - that is, with a two-word combination that has rhymes on both ***light*** and ***year***?

Difficult? Not at all! We just separate the parts of the double-barrelled theme-word and use our rhyme-finding method on each in turn. So ...

Looking for rhyme-words on ***light*** gives:

blight/ bright/ fight/ flight/ fright/ height/ kite/ mite/ might/ night/ plight/ quite/ right/ sight/ slight/ spite/ tight/ white

And rhyme-words on ***year***:

clear/ cheer/ dear/ drear/ ear/ fear/ gear/ hear/ jeer/ leer/ mere/ near/ peer/ pier/ queer/ rear/ seer/ sheer/ smear/ sneer/ spear/ steer/ tear/ veer

... produce rhymes for each word separately, then try them in different combinations.

Now look for a combination that will give a usable rhyme with ***light-year*** - there are no less than 432 possible combinations with the words I've listed, so there should be something there!

How about ***night*** and ***dear*** in a slogan like ...

> *... star thoughts come out each night dear, and don't take a light-year*

Or ***bright*** and ***clear*** in ...

> *... slogans come that are bright, clear, and don't take a light-year ...*

Or ***right*** and ***near*** in ...

> *... the ideas are right near, not away by a light-year*

You've probably spotted more possibilities for yourself.

The point I'm trying to make here is: **don't shy away from challenging rhymes**.

The brainstorming technique will give you plenty of ideas, and if a neat double rhyme really comes off it's very, very effective.

*

**Original:**

> *... It helps my slogans boldly go where no man has gone before*

This is another special. Let me suggest that the **main slogan theme-word(s)** are ***no man*** and then explain why in a moment.

But first, I've anticipated that you recognise the catch-phrase the above slogan is based on. I'm quite confident about this one. There can't be many people who don't recognise the famous introduction to the highly successful 'Star Trek' television programmes.

If this was a real competition though, and you - as a judge - didn't recognise the catchphrase I'm using, then that's it: I'm sunk.

Slogans based on 'well-known' sayings are risky - the judge might not know the saying!

So an absolutely fundamental question that you must ask if ever you think of using this approach with a slogan of your own is: will the judges have heard of the phrase/saying that I'm using? Is it **really** well-known? If there's any doubt in your mind at all, then forget it.

If you do try this approach ...

In this example, I think I'm on pretty safe ground. So, back to my earlier question - why choose ***no man*** to rhyme with?

... aim for a **parody** of the original ...

The reason is that we're not going to leave the famous catchphrase as it is. What we're going to try for is a **parody** - a change that produces a new slogan but still allows you to recognise the famous original. What that means is that you can't change the order of the words in the original; if you do, it won't be recognised, and that's an essential requirement.

... by changing its **subject**.

The other point is that, when changing a well- known phrase, the greatest impact is made if you can change the **subject** of the phrase. That's especially true with a slogan, because what you want to do is to put your own subject in it's place. Now in this case, although ***man*** is the subject, it's so linked to ***no*** in everybody's mind that we can take the two words as inseparable.

So, go for a double rhyme again, on ***no*** and ***man***.

When I did this, I started on a list of **rhyme- words** like this:

bow/ blow/ crow/ flow/ go/ glow/ grow/ hoe/ low/ mow/ row/ so/ show/ slow ...

And I stopped right there. I didn't complete the exercise.

Sometimes you'll do this exercise and the perfect rhyme will jump right up at you. You don't need to go any further, because you know what you've got is right. In this case, I stopped at 'slow'. Why? Because simply saying that word aloud triggered off just the parody that I was looking for. Saying ***slow*** triggered the word ***slogan*** in my mind. And ***slogan***, if said in a slightly forced way - perfectly allowable for a parody - rhymes with ***no man***! So it just had to be:

> *(I think 'How To Write Competition Slogans' is out of this world because ...)*
>
> *... It helps me boldly go where 'slogan' has gone before!*

*

**Original:**

> *... It's the slogan-writers' equivalent of the Big Bang*

Finally ...

The ***main slogan theme-word*** is: ***bang***

This produces **rhyme-words**:

clang/ fang/ gang/ hang/ prang/ rang/ sang/ slang/ tang/ twang

out of which I chose ... none of them. They were all hopeless as far as I could see, and any rhyming slogan using one of them would have been horribly forced.

... Don't be afraid to throw a slogan away if it's no good. Remember ...

**Keep the best - throw the rest!**

But the draft slogan itself really isn't strong enough on its own. So what do we do now. That is easy. Ditch it. Be ruthless, that's another rule to work by. As I said right at the start of this manual, the brainstorming technique will produce more ideas than you know what to do with. You can afford to keep only the best.

So, let's summarise what we've achieved. Taking it step-by-step through a straightforward method we've taken a lead-in of:

> *I think 'How To Write Competition Slogans' is out of this world because ...*

and put together no less than **19** slogans to choose from:

As promised ...

*... It neither hinders nor Mars - but makes dull slogans stars!*

*... there's no better book than it, to help writers 'planet'.*

*... you can shoot for the moon with this slogan-writer's boon*

*... it makes ideas come soon - not once in a blue moon!*

*... it helps take the brake off, and my slogans take off!*

*... my slogans take off, and the prizes I rake-off!*

*... It turns my writing-pad into a slogan launch-pad.*

*... it helps launch my slogans into a prize-winning orbit*

*... I'm not Saturn my backside thinking "what on earth can I write"?*

... the methods you've learnt will produce more slogans than you know what to do with!

*... I don't stare into space 'cos ideas come on apace*

*... Now I write hip slogans instead of staring into space, man*

*... It gives me lots of star ideas, not astro-nought!*

*... More slogans per thought - all stars, not astro-nought!*

*... Slogans, long and short - dozens, not astro-nought!*

*... With the techniques we're taught come endless slogans, not astro-nought!*

*... star thoughts come out each night dear, and don't take a light-year*

*... slogans come that are bright, clear, and don't take a light-year ...*

*... the ideas are right near, not away by a light-year*

*... It helps me boldly go where 'slogan' has gone before!*

So what now? Now you carry out the very last step in the business of slogan-writing. But be prepared. Even this last step may surprise you a little bit.

# 8

## Now put yourself in a judge's position because ...

Before choosing which of your slogans to send in ...

... whatever you may think about your slogans - and, of course, you think they're brilliant - it's the judge who's going to make the decision.

That's why this final step is important. It's aim is to put you, as far as it's possible, in the same situation as the person judging the competition .

So, follow these steps carefully.

1. Write out your final list of slogans on a sheet of paper.

2. Put the competition entry form (or forms if you're going for multiple entries) and any labels etc. into a folder.

... shut them away for a week - or longer!

3. Add your sheet of slogans. And then ...

4. **Put the whole lot into a drawer for a week!**

Yes, a week! Longer if possible. This means you've got to plan ahead so that you don't miss entry deadlines, but it's very important that at this stage you DON'T pick one of your slogans and send it off.

Just try to put yourself in the judges' position and you'll understand why. You're snowed under. Thousands, maybe tens of thousands, of entries are being looked at. The amount of time you can spend looking at a slogan is minimal. Five seconds, ten seconds? Certainly not much. Any slogan that's going to get past you and move on to the later stages of judging has got to make an immediate impact.

**That's** why you don't send anything off for as long as you can. The longer the better, because you're actually **trying to forget them**! And the best way to forget about them, of course, is to get on with writing another set of slogans for another competition!

This is a technique that many writers use, particularly comedy writers and fiction writers. Some book writers say they don't look at what they've written for six months! And why? Because when they come back to read their material again, it strikes them as it would a reader who hadn't seen it before. Jokes that aren't strong enough, characterisation that's too wooden, plot weaknesses - all stand out like a sore thumb.

That way you look at them afresh - just as the judge will.

So, by putting those slogans away and coming back to them a week or so later, you'll be seeing them afresh - **just as a judge will look at them.**

The technique now is to scan them quickly - again, just as a judge is likely to look at them quickly.

Work your way down down your list. Say each slogan out loud, but don't dwell on it. Move on to the next one and say that aloud.

Be aware. You're looking and listening for the slogan **that makes the most immediate impact** on you - because if it strikes you instantly, then the chances are that it will have just the same powerful affect on a judge.

You then pick the one that makes the strongest **immediate** impact ...

When that happens, and it will, **that's when you act!** Don't waste any more time thinking about it. Don't go through the list again and again. Just get that entry form filled in, the slogan written and the whole lot in the post.

... send it in ...

Will it win? Who knows? I make no guarantees, and I'm sure you wouldn't expect me to. At the end of the day, it's all in the lap of the judges.

But, if you've followed the techniques in this manual (or adapted and improved them!) then you can be sure of a few things:

- That your slogan will be one that's avoided all the major pitfalls that would have made it an immediate loser
- That it's got the right message
- That it's built on the right theme-words
- And that it's different enough and catchy enough to attract the judges' attention.

With all these going for you, your slogan will almost certainly be better placed to win than 90% of the competition.

... and the best of luck!

Good luck with the final 10%!

# Books To Help

A bit of research never does any harm. Here's a short list of books that could help in different ways.

### Looking for Words

- ❑ English Dictionary & Roget's Thesaurus ISBN 0 582 89368 2 Available as one volume from WH Smith's. Terrific value.
- ❑ Reader's Digest Reverse Dictionary. (Unique book which gives you related words from a start word - a brainstorm book, in effect. Available only from Reader's Digest shops or mail order)

*

### Classic Slogans

- ❑ Slogans, by Nigel Rees. Published by George Allen & Unwin, 1982. (Classic Slogans)
- ❑ A Book of Slogans and Catchphrases, by Nigel Rees, Unwin Paperbacks, 1984.

*

### Famous Sayings

- ❑ The Concise Oxford Dictionary of Proverbs. Published by Oxford University Press, 1982.
- ❑ The Oxford Dictionary of Quotations. Published by Oxford University Press, 1981.
- ❑ The Penguin Dictionary of Modern Quotations, by J.M. & M.J. Cohen. Published by Penguin Books, 1980.
- ❑ Sayings of the Twentieth Century, by Nigel Rees. Published by George Allen & Unwin, 1984.